How Our Government Works

Frank Schaffer Publications®

Frank Schaffer Publications®

Printed in the United States of America. All rights reserved. Limited Reproduction Permission: Permission to duplicate these materials is limited to the person for whom they are purchased. Reproduction for an entire school or school district is unlawful and strictly prohibited. Frank Schaffer Publications is an imprint of School Specialty Publishing. Copyright © 2008 School Specialty Publishing.

Send all inquiries to:
Frank Schaffer Publications
8720 Orion Place
Columbus, Ohio 43240

How Our Government Works—Grade 5

ISBN 0-7682-3535-9

1 2 3 4 5 6 7 8 9 10 POH 10 09 08

What's It For? ★★★★★★★★★★★★★★★★★★★★★★★★

Government is the people and institutions empowered to make decisions about laws and how they are carried out. Laws deal with many issues and problems, including how resources are distributed, how revenues are collected, and how conflicts are resolved. Below is a list of ideas about how the purposes government should serve. Your task is to rank each idea from "1" for the most important or most acceptable purpose to "10" for the lease important or most unacceptable purpose. Write the reasons for your ranking on the lines provided.

Rank   **Reason**

_____ Protecting the rights of individuals   _____

_____ Providing economic security   _____

_____ Promoting the general welfare   _____

_____ Molding the character of citizens   _____

_____ Furthering the interests of a
        particular group   _____

_____ Promoting a particular religion   _____

_____ Providing military security   _____

_____ Establishing moral principles   _____

_____ Promoting a particular political
        party   _____

_____ Promoting the spread of
        information   _____

Framers of the Constitution ★★★★★★★★★★★★

Before the Philadelphia meeting, in the summer of 1787, the national government, under the Articles of Confederation, was too weak to rule effectively. Because of this, many people were angry and demanded changes. The delegates originally came to Philadelphia to deal with these problems and make recommendations for changes. However, they quickly made the bold decision to write a completely new constitution for the country. The Constitution they wrote, or framed, is the one we have today.

The delegates to the meeting, or *Constitutional Convention* as it is now called, included some of the most famous names in American history. George Washington was elected president of the convention. Many of the delegates were only in their 30s, including James Madison and Alexander Hamilton. The oldest delegate was Benjamin Franklin at 81. James Madison is credited with contributing more to the writing of the Constitution than any of the others, which earned him the title "Father of the Constitution." Over half of the framers were lawyers and judges, a fourth were landowners, all of them had held at least one public office, and all of them were wealthy.

Through the framers differed on many issues, they were a daring and creative group, who were willing to take steps to establish a strong national government. Throughout the summer, the framers debated, wrote, and rewrote the Constitution. Finally, on September 17, 1787, the framers finished their work. The new Constitution proposed a powerful executive and a Senate with powers equal to those of the House of Representatives. Now it was up to the states to accept or reject the Constitution.

1. In what city did the delegates meet?_____

2. How many delegates came to the meeting? _____

3. What kids of backgrounds did the delegates have?_____

4. Why did the delegates meet? _____

5. Did they have an easy job to do? _____

6. Who was the oldest delegate? _____

7. Who was elected president of the meeting? _____

8. What was the meeting called? _____

9. Who was called the "Father of the Constitution"? _____

10. What was the main difference between the Articles of Confederation and the

    Constitution? _____

In Your Own Words ★★★★★★★★★★★★★★★★★

The Preamble to the Constitution of the United States is presented below. After you read the preamble, identify the six purposes of government stated in it. Then, tell what each of these purposes means in your own words.

We the People of the United States, in Order to form a more perfect Union, establish Justice, insure domestic Tranquility, provide for the common defense, promote the general Welfare, and secure the Blessings of Liberty to ourselves and our Posterity, do ordain and establish this Constitution for the United States of America.

The purposes of government, as stated in the Preamble to the Constitution are to

1. _____

    In your own words this means _____

2. _____

    In your own words this means

3. _____

    In your own words this means _____

4. _____

    In your own words this means _____

5. _____

    In your own words this means _____

6. _____

    In your own words this means _____

Amendment Matchup ✭✭✭✭✭✭✭✭✭✭✭✭✭✭✭✭✭

The Framers of the Constitution realized that the needs and circumstances of a society change when they provided for changes in the Constitution. Amendments to the Constitution have either been additions to or change in the original document. Since the Bill of Rights was added to the Constitution in 1791, only 17 amendments have been ratified. Consult a copy of the amendment section of the Constitution to determine what each amendment is about. Then write the amendment's number on the line in front of the statement describing it.

Statements

_____ **A.** Repealed the Eighteenth Amendment

_____ **B.** Described the rights of citizens, representation, and voting

_____ **C.** Stated no one could be kept from voting for not paying taxes

_____ **D.** Did away with slavery

_____ **E.** Gave vote to citizens aged 18 and older

_____ **F.** Gave women the right to vote

_____ **G.** Stated that no person can be elected president more than twice

_____ **H.** Allowed voters to elect senators

_____ **I.** Provided for succession to the presidency and presidential disability

_____ **J.** Stated that no one could be denied the vote because of race, color, or because he was a former slave

_____ **K.** Changed the dates of the president and vice president's term in office

_____ **L.** Prohibited the manufacture and sale of liquor

_____ **M.** Gave citizens who live in Washington, D.C., the right to vote in presidential elections

_____ **N.** Explained what kinds of cases federal courts could try

_____ **O.** Changed how the electoral college worked

_____ **P.** Stated that laws passed to increase the salaries of senators and representatives could not take effect until after an election of representatives had taken place

_____ **Q.** Gave Congress the power to collect taxes on income

Amendments

Amendment 11 (1795)
Amendment 12 (1804)
Amendment 13 (1865)
Amendment 14 (1868)
Amendment 15 (1870)
Amendment 16 (1913)
Amendment 17 (1913)
Amendment 18 (1919)
Amendment 19 (1920)
Amendment 20 (1933)
Amendment 21 (1933)
Amendment 22 (1951)
Amendment 23 (1961)
Amendment 24 (1964)
Amendment 25 (1967)
Amendment 26 (1971)
Amendment 27 (1992)

Amending the Constitution ★★★★★★★★★★★★★★

The Constitution has been a lasting document. Written over 200 years ago, its authors realized times would change so they provided a way the Constitution could be changed when necessary.

1. Which article provides for such changes?

_____

2. What is a change in the Constitution called?

_____

A change to the Constitution may be proposed when either two thirds of Congress or two thirds of the states request it. To be accepted as part of the Constitution, the proposed amendment must be ratified by three fourths of the states. It is not easy to make constitutional changes.

Over 9,000 amendments have been proposed over the years, but only 27 have been ratified by three fourths of the states. Even with popular support from the population at large, such as the Equal Rights Amendment recently had, ratification is not always ensured. Three suggestions for constitutional reform are listed below:

1. Change treaty ratification from two-thirds approval by the Senate to 60 percent.

2. Congress should authorize a limit to campaign spending.

3. Terms for members of the House of Representatives should be four years rather than two.

Citizens-at-large can have input into making changes by writing to their senators and representatives. Select one of the suggestions above. Then write a paragraph expressing your opinion about the suggestion under consideration. Back up your opinions with sound reasoning.

_____

_____

_____

_____

Functions of Government ☆☆☆☆☆☆☆☆☆☆☆☆☆☆

Some functions of government are listed below inside the boxes. For each of the purposes write down on a separate sheet of paper a specific example of how it affects you or someone you know personally.

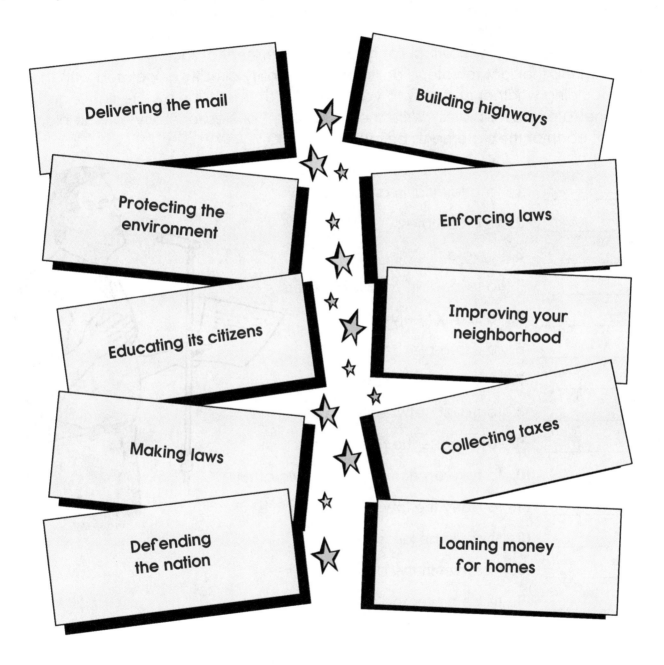

Rights and Responsibilities ✮✮✮✮✮✮✮✮✮✮✮✮

You have probably heard the expression "Get a life!" An important part of your life, both now and in the future, is your civic life. What is your civic life? *Civics* refers to the political rights and responsibilities of citizenship. The word *civics* comes from the Latin word *civis*, which means citizen. *Political rights* are powers or privileges to which all citizens are due or entitled. *Political responsibilities* refer to obligations and actions regarding the exercise of political rights for the betterment of society. An important political right is the right to vote; a political responsibility directly associated with this right is deciding whether and how to vote. Which statements below are rights, and which ones are responsibilities? Write the word "right" or "responsibility" on the blank in front of each of the statements below.

_____ **1.** to a fair trial in a court of law

_____ **2.** to a free press

_____ **3.** to vote

_____ **4.** to respect the rights of others

_____ **5.** to speak freely

_____ **6.** to assemble

_____ **7.** to criticize the government

_____ **8.** to travel between states

_____ **9.** to exercise the right to vote

_____ **10.** to take an active part in civic affairs

_____ **11.** to obey the laws

_____ **12.** to serve on juries

_____ **13.** to server in the armed forces

_____ **14.** to be protected from hate speech

_____ **15.** to write a letter to the editor

_____ **16.** to pay taxes

_____ **17.** to petition the government

Name _____ Date _____

Democratic Quiz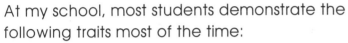

Below are some traits that are important to the preservation and improvement of American democracy. Circle the score that best describes students are your school.

3=very true for your school
2=somewhat true for your school
1=not at all true for your school

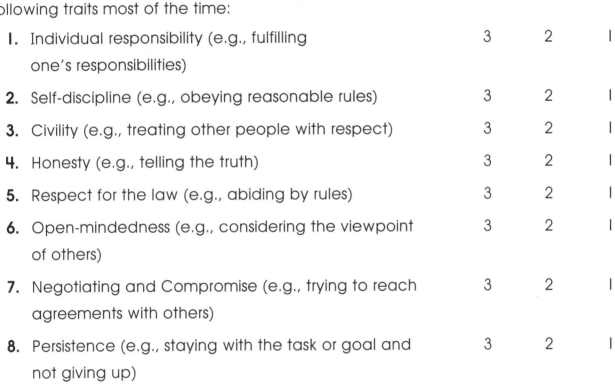

At my school, most students demonstrate the following traits most of the time:

1.	Individual responsibility (e.g., fulfilling one's responsibilities)	3	2	1
2.	Self-discipline (e.g., obeying reasonable rules)	3	2	1
3.	Civility (e.g., treating other people with respect)	3	2	1
4.	Honesty (e.g., telling the truth)	3	2	1
5.	Respect for the law (e.g., abiding by rules)	3	2	1
6.	Open-mindedness (e.g., considering the viewpoint of others)	3	2	1
7.	Negotiating and Compromise (e.g., trying to reach agreements with others)	3	2	1
8.	Persistence (e.g., staying with the task or goal and not giving up)	3	2	1
9.	Civic-mindedness (e.g., showing concern for one's community and nation)	3	2	1
10.	Compassion (e.g., concern for the well-being of others)	3	2	1
11.	Patriotism (e.g., loyalty to the values and principles underlying the American constitutional democracy)	3	2	1

Protecting Your Rights ★★★★★★★★★★★★★★★

Due process refers to the right of every citizen to be protected from unlawful and/or abusive actions by government. The major due process protections are listed on the right. A definition of each protection is listed on the left. Use classroom and library resources to correctly match them.

Definition	Protection
_____ 1. Every person accused of a crime must be represented by an attorney.	**A.** habeas corpus
_____ 2. A group of individuals are chosen to make a decision about the guilt or innocence of an accused person.	**B.** presumption of innocence
_____ 3. A court of justice must be comprised of objective and fair-minded officials.	**C.** fair notice
_____ 4. This principle ensures that a person found not guilty cannot be tried again on the same charges.	**D.** impartial tribunal
_____ 5. An accused person has a right to be informed of the charges against him/her.	**E.** speedy and public trials
_____ 6. A person accused of a crime is still considered to be free from guilt until proven otherwise in a court of law.	**F.** right to counsel
_____ 7. An accused person does not have to give evidence that could be used against him or her.	**G.** trial by jury.
_____ 8. A person found guilty of a crime can ask a higher court to rehear his or her case.	**H.** right against self-incrimination
_____ 9. A person accused of a crime has the right to be brought to trial as quickly as possible in a court room that is open to the public.	**I.** protection against double jeopardy
_____ 10. The court order demands that the person in custody be brought to court and shown the reasons for detention.	**J.** right of appeal

Name _____   Date _____

Citizen Checklist ⭐⭐⭐⭐⭐⭐⭐⭐⭐⭐⭐⭐⭐⭐⭐⭐⭐⭐⭐

Below is a list of questions. A good citizen
needs to know how the answers to these
questions. How many do you know? Write
the answers on the line under each question.
If you do not know the answer, ask your
parents or another adult to help you.

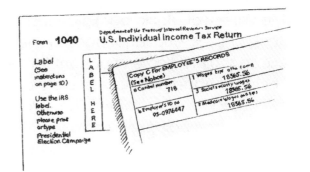

I. How do you apply for a
   Social Security card?

   _____

2. How do you get legal advice?

   _____

3. How, and to whom, do you report a crime?

   _____

4. How do you sign up to vote?

   _____

5. How do you find your polling place?

   _____

6. How do you file a tax return?

   _____

7. How do you find out what the minimum wage is?

   _____

8. Where do you go, and what do you need to know, to get a driver's license?

   _____

American Society ✮✮✮✮✮✮✮✮✮✮✮✮✮✮✮✮✮

A wide variety of ethnic backgrounds, races, religions, classes, and languages shape American society. Some important factors that helped shape American society are listed below. Research each factor. Then write down inside the box a reason why each factor was important.

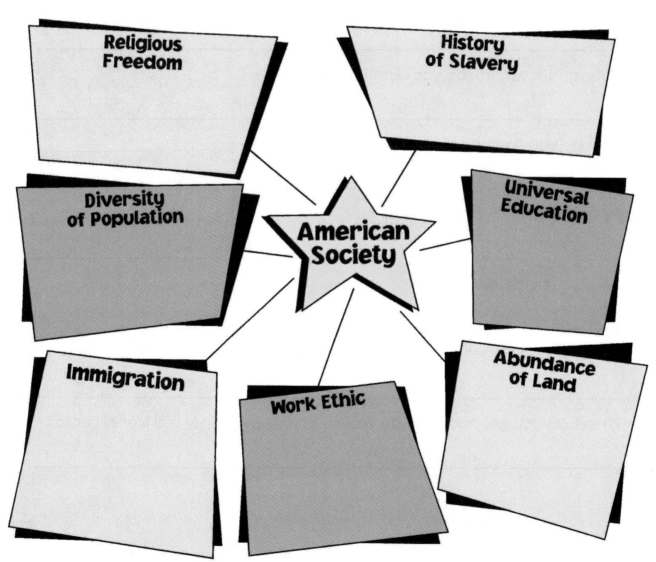

Religious
Freedom

History
of Slavery

Diversity
of Population

American
Society

Universal
Education

Immigration

Work Ethic

Abundance
of Land

16   *How Our Government Works: Grade 5*

Name _____   Date _____

Who Represents You? ★★★★★★★★★★★★★★★★★★

Few Americans can identify the key people elected to serve them. Who represents
you in the legislative and executive branches of your local, state, and national
governments? Find out, and write their names under each title.

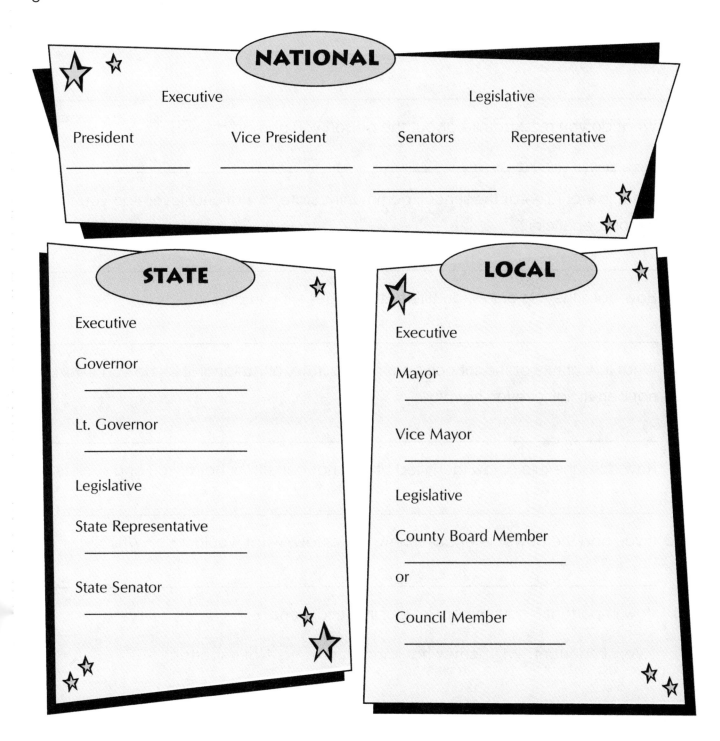

NATIONAL

Executive   Legislative

President   Vice President   Senators   Representative

_____   _____   _____   _____

                                      _____

STATE

Executive

Governor

_____

Lt. Governor

_____

Legislative

State Representative

_____

State Senator

_____

LOCAL

Executive

Mayor

_____

Vice Mayor

_____

Legislative

County Board Member

_____

or

Council Member

_____

Name _____   Date _____

Government in Your Life ✫✫✫✫✫✫✫✫✫✫✫✫✫✫

To examine the influence government has on you, answer the questions below.
After you complete the questionnaire, pair up with another student and compare
your answers.

1. Who is your favorite and most admired leader in American government,
    past or present?

    _____

2. What do you most admire about the person you named above?

    _____

3. What law or rule—at the school, community, state, or national level—do you think
    is most beneficial?

    _____

4. How does the rule or law identified above benefit you and society?

    _____

5. What law or rule at the school, community, state, or national level do you think is
    not beneficial, or even harmful?

    _____

6. How does the rule or law identified above not benefit, or harm, you and society?

    _____

7. If you had the power to enact a new rule or law, what would it be? Why?

    _____

8. How important is government in your life (circle one)?

    Very important   Somewhat important   Not important

Forms of Government ✮✮✮✮✮✮✮✮✮✮✮✮✮✮✮✮✮

There are different ways to classify governments. With a system to classify governments, you can better compare and analyze them. Read the following two ways to classify governments. Then, answer the questions below.

Confederal, Federal, and Unitary Governments

The relationship between the central government of a nation and other units of government can be classified as confederal, federal, and unitary systems. In a *confederal system* each state is sovereign. This means that each state hast he right to rule itself, except for powers delegated to the central government for specific purposes. Examples of the confederal system are the United States under the Articles of Confederation and the Confederate States of America. In a federal system powers are divided and shared between the national and state governments. An example is the government of the United States under the U.S. Constitution. In a unitary system, power is concentrated in the central government. The 50 states and hundreds of local governments that can exercise only those powers given them by the central government are examples of unitary systems.

Presidential and Parliamentary Government

Another way to classify governments is based on the relationship between the legislative and executive branches. The United States has a presidential system (also called a system of *shared powers*) in which the powers are separated between two branches. the president and vice president are chosen by all of the people every four years. Legislators are chosen by people within states and districts. In contrast, in a parliamentary system, such as Great Britain's, the prime minister, who is the chief executive officer, is chosen from among the ranks of the majority party in parliament. (Note: *parliament* is another name for "legislature".)

1. How do presidential and parliamentary governments differ?

   _____

   _____

2. What are the characteristics of confederal, federal, and unitary governments?

   _____

   _____

Name _____   Date _____

Community Needs ★★★★★★★★★★★★★★★★★★★★

Imagine you have been elected to city council.
As a city council board member, it is your
responsibility to fight for the needs of your district.
below is a list of proposals for meeting those
needs. Although it would be nice to do everything
on the list, the city can afford to only do a few of
them. The city has a total of $1 million to spend. Your task is to identify proposals that
you personally believe are the most important to fund by ranking them from 1 for
the most important to 12 for the least important. The cost for each proposal is in the
parentheses. Remember you cannot spend more than $1 million, so consider the
different needs carefully. After you rank the proposals, discuss your rankings with
another student.

_____ buy land for a new park ($500,000)

_____ build a new parking lot ($300,000)

_____ add ten members to the police force ($200,000)

_____ provide day-care services for the needy ($100,000)

_____ fund a baseball park ($700,000)

_____ build another elementary school ($800,000)

_____ add a wing to the hospital ($400,000)

_____ build low-income housing ($1,000,000)

_____ develop a mass transit bus system ($400,000)

_____ expand the library ($500,000)

_____ buy a new fire truck ($300,000)

_____ build a produce/fruit/vegetable market ($100,000)

Asking the Right Questions ★★★★★★★★★★★★★★

to make wise decisions, you must ask the right questions. For example, if you are trying to decide which shirt to buy, you would probably ask yourself questions like "How much do the shirts cost?" and "Which shirt do I like the best?" Good citizens also must ask the right questions about local, state, and national issues. List four questions that you would want to ask for each of the issues described below.

Issue #1—The city board is debating about whether or not to create a nature center.

Questions:

1. _____
2. _____
3. _____
4. _____

Issue #2—Members of a Rifle and Hunter's Club want to use the school's auditorium for a Saturday meeting and firearms exhibit.

Questions:

1. _____
2. _____
3. _____
4. _____

Issue #3—The school board debates changing from a 9-month to a 12-month school year.

Questions:

1. _____
2. _____
3. _____
4. _____

Name _____ Date _____

Community Resources ✮✮✮✮✮✮✮✮✮✮✮✮✮✮✮

A good citizen is aware of the resources available in his/her community. Use a local telephone book to find the services listed below. Name the organization/service and a local phone number on the lines provided.

Drug abuse and addiction information and treatment

_____

_____

Social service organizations

_____

_____

Health department

_____

_____

Human services

_____

_____

Parks and recreation

_____

_____

Voter registration

_____

_____

Minority programs and affirmative action

_____

_____

Economic development

_____

_____

A Federal System ☆☆☆☆☆☆☆☆☆☆☆☆☆☆☆☆☆☆☆☆

The U.S. Constitution created a federal government—a system that divided powers between national government and the state governments. In some areas, the national government had control, and in other areas, each of the 50 states had control. For each of the powers listed below, write N on the blank if it is controlled by the national government and S on the blank if it is controlled by the state governments. Consult a copy of the U.S. Constitution in a resource book to make certain your answers are correct.

_____ 1. War is declared.

_____ 2. A tax is placed on goods coming in the United States from foreign countries.

_____ 3. Money is provided to repair state roads.

_____ 4. A treaty is made between the United States and another country.

_____ 5. A new stamp is designed.

_____ 6. Speed limits on rural roads are established.

_____ 7. A child must be a certain age before entering school.

_____ 8. The election date for state officials is set.

_____ 9. Money is allotted to build a new aircraft carrier for the U.S. Navy.

_____ 10. Money is printed.

_____ 11. Rules are established for becoming a U.S. citizen.

_____ 12. A license is issued to drive an automobile.

_____ 13. A post office is built in town.

_____ 14. A person is fined for running a red light.

_____ 15. Salaries for the president and vice president are raised.

_____ 16. Children must attend school until they reach a certain age.

_____ 17. The number of immigrants allowed to come to the United States is increased.

_____ 18. A person goes to trial for spying on the U.S. Government.

Branches of Government ☆☆☆☆☆☆☆☆☆☆☆☆☆☆

The powers of the national government are distributed among the legislative, executive, and judicial branches. Use library resources to identify the power of the three branches. List the power below inside the appropriate box.

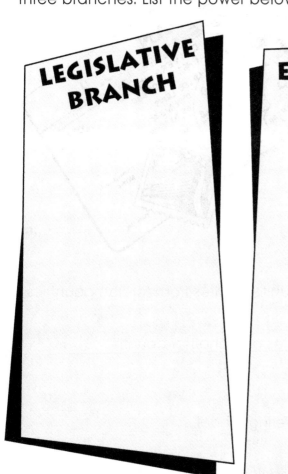

- impeach the government

- nominate members of the federal judiciary

- pass laws over the president's veto by two-thirds majority vote of both Houses

- establish committees to oversee activities of executive branch

- overrule decisions made by lower courts

- disapprove appointments made by the president

- declare laws made by Congress to be unconstitutional

- veto laws passed by Congress

- declare actions of the executive branch to be unconstitutional

- propose amendments to the U.S. Constitution

Name _____   Date _____

Organization of the U.S. Government ☆☆☆☆☆☆

Below is a list of names of various positions, departments, agencies, and groups that operate within the three branches of the United States Government. Your job is to match the name with the correct branch. For each one, place either an E for executive branch, J for judicial branch, or L for legislative branch on the blank in front of each number.

_____ 1. President

_____ 2. Chief Justice

_____ 3. Speaker

_____ 4. Vice President

_____ 5. Senate

_____ 6. House of Representatives

_____ 7. Supreme Court

_____ 8. White House Office

_____ 9. Cabinet

_____ 10. Courts of Appeals

_____ 11. National Security Council

_____ 12. Library of Congress

_____ 13. General Accounting Office

_____ 14. District Courts

_____ 15. Government Printing Office

_____ 16. Secretary of State

_____ 17. Tax Court

_____ 18. U.S. Botanical Gardens

_____ 19. Sentencing Commission

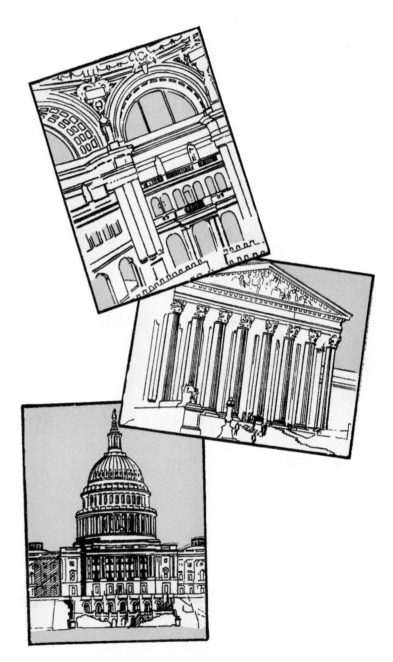

Domestic Policies ✮✮✮✮✮✮✮✮✮✮✮✮✮✮✮✮✮✮✮

The national government has many major responsibilities for domestic policies. *Domestic* refers to policies related and limited to one's own country. These policies have significant consequences for all Americans. On the left side of the chart below is a list of important domestic policies. Examples of both historical and current policies are included. Your task is to investigate each policy using resources from the classroom and library. Then explain how and why each of these policies affects the daily lives of Americans, both past and present.

Policy	Effects of Policy
1. Pure Food and Drug Act	_____
2. Environmental Protection Act	_____
3. civil rights laws	_____
4. child labor laws	_____
5. minimum wage laws	_____
6. Social Security	_____
7. Medicare	_____

Name _____ Date _____

Foreign Policy ☆☆☆☆☆☆☆☆☆☆☆☆☆

Below are listed some historical and contemporary examples of important U.S. government foreign policies. Use classroom and library resources to learn about them. Then briefly describe the significant consequences of each policy on the daily lives of people.

Foreign Policy   **Consequences**

1. Monroe Doctrine _____

_____

2. Marshall Plan _____

_____

3. Truman Doctrine _____

_____

4. immigration acts _____

_____

5. foreign aid _____

_____

6. arms control _____

_____

7. human rights _____

_____

Name _____ Date _____

All About the House ★★★★★★★★★★★★★★★★★★

A democratic government needs a legislative body that represents the people. One of the two law-making bodies established as a result of the Great Compromise at the Constitutional Convention was the House of Representatives. The House, as it is often called, is the larger of the two chambers of Congress. Use classroom and library resources to correctly match the items from Lists One and Two. Write the letter from List Two that corresponds to the correct identification on the blank provided.

List One

_____ 1. another name for House of Representatives

_____ 2. term of service is ____ years

_____ 3. total number of representatives allowed

_____ 4. leader of House

_____ 5. The number of representatives per state is based on ____.

_____ 6. ____ has more representatives than any other state.

_____ 7. every state has at least this many representatives

_____ 8. minimum age to be eligible for election to House

_____ 9. Every ten years, a ____ is conducted, which may result in the reapportionment of a state's number of representatives.

_____ 10. Of the two bodies of Congress, only the House of Representatives can introduce bills that deal with ____.

List Two

A. population

B. two

C. one

D. four

E. lower house

F. General Assembly

G. census

H. 435

I. 268

J. speaker

K. Whip

L. texas

M. California

N. taxes

O. treaties

P. 25

Q. 30

Name _____   Date _____

Senate Facts ✫✫✫✫✫✫✫✫✫✫✫✫✫✫✫✫✫✫✫✫✫

Use your research skills to track down the facts that are missing from the passage below. You can use any source you can find to complete the passage.

Compared to the House, the other law-making body of Congress, the Senate is much

_____ (1). The Senate is composed of _____ (2) members from each

_____ (3). Therefore, the total number of senators is _____ (4). Another name

for the Senate is the _____ (5). The Senate can introduce all kinds of legislation

except _____ (6) bills. Only the Senate can approve or reject _____ (7) and

certain presidential _____ (8) for government positions, such as judges for federal

courts. Originally the Constitution gave each state _____ (9) the power to select

the senators from each state, but that was changed in 1913 by the _____ (10)

Amendment, which gave the _____ (11) the right to elect them. A senator serves

a _____ (12) -year term. no senators are elected at the same time from one

_____ (13).

The only duty given the vice president in the _____ (14) is that of _____ (15)

of the Senate. The vice president presides over sessions of the Senate, but may vote

only in the case of a _____ (16). The senators choose a _____ (17) from their

membership to preside over the sessions when the vice president cannot be there.

Comparing Houses of Congress ★★★★★★★★★★★

Use classroom and library resources to compare and contrast the structure and functions of the Senate and House of Representatives. Write the information on the chart below.

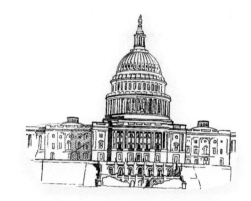

	Senate	House of Representatives
Number of members		
How elected		
Title of members		
Constituents represented		
Qualifications: age, citizenship, & residence		
Length of term		
Title of presiding officer		
Name of current presiding officer		
Impeachment power		
Unique responsibilities		

Making Laws ☆☆☆☆☆☆☆☆☆☆☆☆☆☆☆☆☆☆☆☆☆☆

Both senators and representatives may introduce bills, but only members of the House may introduce bills that deal with taxes or spending. Both house of Congress must pass identical versions of a bill before it can become law. Once a bill is introduced in either house, it goes through almost the same process. After a bill has been approved by Congress, it is sent to the president who may do one of several things. The different steps, from 1 through 9, that make up the process are listed in random order below. use resource books to help you arrange the steps in correct order from first to last. Write a 1 on the blank in front of the first step, 2 on the blank in front of the second step, etc., through step 9.

_____ **A.** President signs bill (or, alternatively, does not act on a bill within ten-day period after receiving it) and it becomes law, or president vetoes bill (or, alternatively does not act on a bill within ten-day period after receiving it, but Congress adjourns before ten-day period is up), and it is returned to the House.

_____ **B.** Both houses agree on the bill, and it is signed by the speaker and vice president.

_____ **C.** Committee releases the bill for the entire House's consideration.

_____ **D.** Bill is passed by either house.

_____ **E.** Bill is introduced and assigned to a committee.

_____ **F.** Bill is sent to the other house for input and consideration.

_____ **G.** Congress makes changes in bill to satisfy president's wishes, and it is returned to president who then signs it, or two thirds of both houses vote for it as it is and the bill becomes a law despite the president's veto.

_____ **H.** Differences between two houses are worked out by a joint conference committee.

_____ **I.** Bill is sent to president for his/her signature.

The Judicial Branch ★★★★★★★★★★★★★★★★★★

The Supreme Court heads the judicial branch of the
United States government. It is the only court established
by the Constitution.

The Supreme Court usually makes decisions of national
importance. The court acts within the laws stated by the
Constitution. Because the wording of the Constitution is
sometimes hard to understand, it can be difficult to interpret
the law. That is one of the duties of the Supreme Court.
When the court does make a decision, all other courts in the country
must follow that decision to guarantee equal legal justice to all
Americans. The Constitution also give the Supreme Court the power to
judge whether federal, state, and local governments are acting within
the law and also to decide if an action of the president is constitutional.

Answer the questions below. The letters in boxes in the answers when
unscrambled will spell out what a judge in the Supreme Court is called.

1. The Supreme Court usually only   __ __ ☐ __ __ __ __ __
    hears what kind of cases?

2. What set of laws guides the Supreme Court's decisions?

    __ __ __   __ __ __ ☐ __ __ __ ☐ __ __ __ __

3. The Supreme Court heads what branch   ☐ __ __ __ __ ☐ __ __
    of government?

4. What other courts are there in the United States   __ __ __ ☐ __ __ __
    that must follow the decisions of
    the Supreme Court?   __ __ __ __ __   __ __ ☐ __ __

5. What is a judge that sits on the
    Supreme Court bench called?   __ __ __ __ __ __ __

The Supreme Court ★★★★★★★★★★★★★★★★★★

The Supreme Court is the only court created by the Constitution. Nine justices sit on the Supreme Court, including the chief justice. The justices are appointed by the president for life. It is their job to hear the most important and often the most controversial cases in the land. It can hear cases involving disputed between states or when a foreign country is involved. Most of the cases are appeals or requests to review lower court rulings. Each year, thousands of petitions (requests to hear appeals) are sent to the Supreme Court. Only a few of these are actually heard by the court. At least four justices must agree before a petition can be heard. After a case is argued before the court, the justices vote on it. At least five votes one way or the other are required to reach a decision. Once a decision is reached, the ruling is written up. Past rulings are used to guide future decisions in similar cases. Since the Supreme Court is the court of last appeal, its decisions are final and must be followed by all other courts.

Below are descriptions of two actual Supreme Court cases. If you had been one of the justices, how would you have voted?

1. Mr. Gideon, who was arrested for petty larceny, asked the court to appoint a lawyer to represent him. His request was turned down, and Gideon represented himself. He lost the case and was sentenced to prison. While in prison, he petitioned the Supreme Court to hear his case, arguing that since he did not have a court-appointed lawyer, he did not have a fair trial. What do you think?

   _____

   _____

2. Mr. Wong was born in California to parents who were both citizens of China. When he returned from a brief visit to China, U.S. Government immigration officials refused to readmit him to this country. They claimed he was not a U.S. citizen because the Fourteenth Amendment did not apply in this case. What do you think?

   _____

   _____

Name _____ Date _____

Important Supreme Court Decisions ★★★★★★

Some important Supreme Court cases are described on the left below. The names of the cases are listed on the right. Match the case with its name by writing the correct letter on the blank in front of the number.

Cases

_____ 1. The court established the power to review acts of Congress and declare laws unconstitutional if they violate the Constitution.

_____ 2. The court declared the Missouri Compromise of 1820 unconstitutional.

_____ 3. The court ruled that the Bills of Rights applied to the states.

_____ 4. The court ruled that separate schools for blacks and whites were inherently unequal.

_____ 5. The court ruled that a woman's decision to have an abortion should be left to her and her physician.

_____ 6. The court ruled that the president did not have temporary immunity from lawsuit from actions not related to official duties.

_____ 7. The court ruled that suspects of a crime must be informed of their rights.

_____ 8. The court ruled that separate but equal facilities for blacks and whites on trains did not violate civil rights of blacks.

_____ 9. The court ruled that neither the states nor Congress could limit the terms of members of Congress.

_____ 10. The court ruled that school officials could not require a pupil to recite a state-composed prayer.

Name

A. *Miranda v. Arizona,* 1966

B. *Brown v. Board of Education,* 1954

C. *Clinton v. Jones,* 1997

D. *Roe v. Wade,* 1973

E. *Marbury v. Madison,* 1803

F. *Gitlow v. New York,* 1925

G. *U.S. Term Limits Inc, v. Thorton,* 1995

H. *Engel v. Vitale,* 1962

I. *Dred Scott v. Sanford,* 1857

J. *Plessy v. Ferguson,* 1896

The Executive Branch ✩✩✩✩✩✩✩✩✩✩✩✩✩✩✩✩✩

The president heads the executive branch of the United States. In Article II of the Constitution, the duties of the president are stated.

1. In Section I, paragraph I of that article it states the length of the president's term. What is it?

   _____

2. Who else is elected at the same time and for the same time period?

   _____

3. What are the three qualifications a person must have to be the president?

   _____

   _____

   _____

4. Section 2 of the above Article states what the president's duties are. Place a check mark next to the duties give to the president by the Constitution.

   _____ **a.** The president may make treaties by himself.

   _____ **b.** The president appoints the vice president.

   _____ **c.** The president is commander in chief of the armed forces.

   _____ **d.** The president makes appointments of ambassadors with the approval of the Senate.

   _____ **e.** The president sees that the federal laws are carried out as they are designed.

   _____ **f.** The president does not tell Congress what he wants.

   _____ **g.** The president has the Congress greet visiting ambassadors.

   _____ **h.** The president may make treaties with the approval of the Senate.

   _____ **i.** The president commissions officers in the armed forces.

5. On a separate piece of paper, write to oath a president must take before entering the presidency—Article II, Section I, paragraph 8.

The Job of the President ☆☆☆☆☆☆☆☆☆☆☆☆☆

The president of the United States has a big job. He is the leader of a whole nation. His decisions affect people in other countries too. How does he know what to do?

The *Constitution* is like a rule book for our country. It explains the president's job. It gives him three main duties. He is our chief *diplomat*. He is the head of our *armed forces*. He is the *enforcer* of our laws.

Chief Diplomat

The president meets with leaders of other countries. He attends fancy dinners and speaks at important meetings. He chooses people to *represent* our nation in other lands. He makes *treaties* with other countries.

Head of Armed Forces

The president talks to leaders of our military. He is their boss. He sends troops to battle. He calls them home again.

Enforcer of Laws

The president chooses top judges. The judges explain laws and the Constitution. They oversee court cases. The president chooses his *cabinet members* or advisors. These trusted workers give advice. The president is also in charge of our police force. In some cases, he even *pardons* crimes. The president often addresses *Congress*. He suggests new ideas. He signs some *bills* into law. He *vetoes* others.

Before being allowed to assume the office of President of the United States, all of our presidents promise to do the best they can at their job. It is a challenging and important promise. Is it a promise you would like to make one day?

Name _____ Date _____

The Job of the President ★★★★★★★★★★★★★★★★

Use five of the following vocabulary words in a paragraph of your own.

Constitution—the basic law of our land
diplomat—a person whose job is to speak to leaders of other countries for us
armed forces—soldiers
enforcer—one who makes sure things are done
represent—stand for
treaties—agreements between countries
cabinet members—people who help the president make decisions
pardons—excuses someone from a crime
bills—the rough draft of a suggested law
veto—the power to stop a bill from becoming a law

Questions to Consider

1. What are the three main duties of the president of the United States?

   _____

   _____

2. What does the president do as chief diplomat of our nation?

   _____

   _____

3. What does the president do as head of our armed forces?

   _____

   _____

4. What are some of the duties of the president as enforcer of laws?

   _____

   _____

5. Would you like to be the president of the United States? Why or why not?

   _____

   _____

6. Which parts of the job would you enjoy? Which parts of the job would you not like?

   _____

   _____

Presidential Power ★★★★★★★★★★★★★★★★★★

Every four years the president takes the Oath of Office. With the responsibility of running the government comes the power that could be misused. The Framers of the Constitution tried to avoid any misuse of presidential power by creating three branches of government—the Legislative, Judicial, and Executive—to check on one another. This system of checks and balances has worked most of the time.

Use the Constitution to help you see how much power the president has been given. Then mark the following statements true or false. Write a "T" or "F" on the blank provided.

_____ **1.** The president is the commander in chief of the armed forces.

_____ **2.** The president may declare war.

_____ **3.** The president has the power to grant reprieved and pardons for offenses against the United States, except in the case of impeachment.

_____ **4.** The president has the power to appoint any official to his cabinet.

_____ **5.** The War Powers Act was passed so that Congress and the president act together in declaring any act of hostility.

_____ **6.** The president is to keep the Congress informed with the State of the Union messages from time to time.

_____ **7.** A treaty must receive two-thirds approval from from the Senate before it is effective.

_____ **8.** The president may recommend legislation.

_____ **9.** The president may introduce legislation.

_____ **10.** The president may make treaties.

_____ **11.** The president must see that the laws are executed.

_____ **12.** The president does not need to consult with anyone but his cabinet when he wants a law passed.

_____ **13.** The president must sign legislations for it to become law.

_____ **14.** Congress passed the National Emergencies Act in 1976 to keep the president's power in check.

_____ **15.** If a president does not want a law passed, he throws away the bill when Congress sends it to him.

_____ **16.** The president can prevent any bill from becoming law unless Congress passes it over his veto.

_____ **17.** The president's cabinet and office can pass laws.

_____ **18.** The president always does what his advisors recommend.

Presidency Fill-In ★★★★★★★★★★★★★★★★★★★

Use the Word Bank at the bottom of the page to fill in the missing words in the paragraphs that follow. All answers will not be used.

As the _____ (1) of the United States, the president helps shape and _____ (2) laws, directs _____ (3) policy, is responsible for national _____ (4), presides at certain ceremonial affairs, and leads his _____ (5).

The president does not control the legislative and _____ (6) branches, but can influence lawmaking and does appoint _____ (7) to the Supreme Court. Since no one person can assume all of the presidential duties, assistants are appointed to carry them out. They form the _____ (8) Office. These individuals advice the president on various matters. The _____ (9), consisting of 14 department heads, called secretaries, is also appointed to advise and assist the president. Cabinet members must be approved by _____ (10).

The president is elected to a _____ (11) -year term, No person can be elected to the office of the president more than _____ (12).

Word Bank

legislative	cabinet	judicial
enforce	party	Congress
foreign	House of Representatives	defense
four	six	twice
chief executive	White House	justices
Supreme Court	Capitol	Speaker
Once		

Cabinet Officers ✮✮✮✮✮✮✮✮✮✮✮✮✮✮✮✮✮✮

The cabinet is an informal group that advises the president. The cabinet consists of the heads of 14 executive departments. The president appoints the heads of the departments, subject to confirmation, or approval, by the Senate. Use a current almanac or other source to identify the current heads of each department. Then write their names on the appropriate blanks below.

Department	Name of Head of Department
1. Secretary of State	_____
2. Secretary of the Treasury	_____
3. Secretary of Defense	_____
4. Attorney General	_____
5. Secretary of the Interior	_____
6. Secretary of Agriculture	_____
7. Secretary of Commerce	_____
8. Secretary of Labor	_____
9. Secretary of Health and Human Services	_____
10. Secretary of Housing and Urban Development	_____
11. Secretary of Transportation	_____
12. Secretary of Energy	_____
13. Secretary of Education	_____
14. Secretary of Veterans Affairs	_____

Name _____ Date _____

Checks and Balances Chart ★★★★★★★★★★★★★

Use classroom and library resources to fill in the chart below. Some boxes will not be filled in.

Power	How It Can Be checked		
	The President may	The Supreme Court may	Congress may
If Congress passes a law, then...			
If the president vetoes a bill passed by Congress, then...			
If the president appoints a Supreme Court judge, then...			
If a federal judge shows misconduct in office, then...			
If the president makes a treaty with another country, then...			
If the president enforces an unjust law, then...			
If the president asks for money for defense, then...			

Powerful Ideas ✩✩✩✩✩✩✩✩✩✩✩✩✩✩✩✩✩✩✩✩

When the Framers of the Constitution assembled in Philadelphia in 1787, they dealt with some very powerful ideas, which are listed in the column on the right. Match the ideas with their correct definitions, which are presented on the left column. Write the letter on the line in front of the number.

Definitions

_____ 1. a proposal for a two-house legislation with representatives in both houses based on each state's population

_____ 2. government by the people

_____ 3. a government regulated by a written or unwritten statement of principles and functions

_____ 4. division of governmental powers between the legislative, executive, and judicial branches

_____ 5. a proposal for a two-house legislature that gave equal representation to one house (Senate) and representation based on population in the other house (House of Representatives)

_____ 6. a two-house form of government

_____ 7. a proposal for a single-house form of legislature with equal representation

_____ 8. a government in which citizens elect officials to represent them

_____ 9. a government in which power is divided between states and a central authority

_____ 10. a division of governmental powers in which each branch has some control and influence over the power of the others

Powerful Idea

A. Republic

B. Separation of Power

C. New Jersey Plan

D. Connecticut Plan

E. Virginia Plan

F. Federalism

G. Democracy

H. Bicameralism

I. Constitutional Government

J. Checks and Balances

A Limited and Unlimited Government ✭✭✭✭✭✭✭

The federal, state, and local governments of the United States are characterized by legal limits on their power. They basis for these limits is set forth in the U.S. Constitution and in the state constitutions. They include institutional devices like "checks and balances" and "bill of rights" and "separation of powers." In contrast, governments with unlimited power over their citizens are nonconstitutional governments in which power is in the hands of one person or a small group. A historical example of

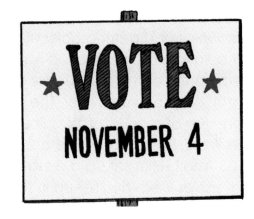

an unlimited government was Nazi Germany under Adolf Hitler. At the bottom of the page are characteristics of limited and unlimited governments, as well as historical and contemporary examples of nations with either limited or unlimited governments. Your task is to write the characteristics and examples inside the correct box.

Limited Government	Unlimited Government

Characteristics:
- regular and free elections
- independent judiciaries
- courts controlled by leader
- protection of individual rights
- no restraints on government
- no free elections
- protection from government
- multiple political parties
- laws apply to leaders as well as the governed
- government use of intimidation and terror
- goals and means of government cannot violate constitution

Nations:
Great Britain
Canada
Soviet Union
France
Iran
Libya
Italy under Mussolini
Myanmar
China

Dictatorships and Democracies ✮✮✮✮✮✮✮✮✮✮

After you read the following information about
dictatorships and democracies, fill in the comparison
chart below. A *dictatorship* is a nation whose
government is completely under the control of a
dictator, or all-powerful ruler. The twentieth century
saw the rise of many dictatorships. Near the end of
World War I, Russian became a Communist dictatorship.
In 1933 Adolf Hitler set up a dictatorship in Germany.
Dictatorships were also set up in Italy, Spain, and most of
the Balkan nations. Although dictatorships may have written
constitutions and elections, the constitutions do not give
freedom to their people, and the elections are controlled by the government. In a
dictatorship, people are not allowed to disagree with the government. The idea of
individual rights is not valued in a dictatorship. Instead, individuals are valued only to the
extent they can serve the government. Democracies are the opposite of dictatorships.
Democratic government is considered to be the servant of the people, rather than the
other way around. Democracies are based on the idea that the people rule. Authority to
govern comes from the people. In a democracy, fair and free elections are held
regularly. Without an informed and questioning citizenry, a democracy could not survive.

Comparing Dictatorships and Democracies

Characteristics of Government	Dictatorships	Democracies
Condition of the People		
Political Process		
Dictatorships		
Democracies		
Status of Individual		

Comparative Governments ✮✮✮✮✮✮✮✮✮✮✮✮✮

Facts about some major foreign governments are presented on the left. A list of nations is on the right. Match the nation with the appropriate information by writing the correct letter on the blank in front of the number.

Facts

____ 1. has 650 members in the House of Commons

____ 2. The legislative branch is called the *Riksdag*.

____ 3. has a president and a parliament elected by people

____ 4. The Communist Party rules the country.

____ 5. Parliament consists of a single-chamber House of Representatives.

____ 6. The government's legal system is based on the teachings of Islam.

____ 7. The parliament is called the *Knesset*.

____ 8. Nelson Mandela was the first black person to be elected president.

____ 9. The parliament is called the *National Diet*.

____ 10. The seat of government is in Moscow.

____ 11. Parliament consists of the House of Commons and Senate.

____ 12. It is called the most democratic nation in Central America.

Nations

A. Costa Rica

B. Japan

C. Russia

D. New Zealand

E. Britain

F. France

G. South Africa

H. China

I. Sweden

J. Saudi Arabia

K. Canada

L. Israel

Write a brief description of one of the governments above.

_____

_____

_____

_____

The United States and the World ★★★★★★★★★

Because the United States is part of an interconnected world, Americans are affected by other nations and other nations are influenced by American policies and society. Six of the most important ways that nations interact with one another are listed below. Search through newspapers and magazines for international news stories related to each of the types of interaction listed below. Then, after you have read the stories, use the information to fill in facts related to the United States and another nation of your choice for each means of interaction.

Types of Interaction	United States	_____ (Write name of nation)
Trade		
Diplomacy		
Treaties and Agreements		
Humanitarian aid		
Economic aid and sanctions		
Military force and the threat of force		

Name _____ Date _____

The Meaning of Democracy ★★★★★★★★★★★

The American system of government is based upon the concept of *democracy*. What does this word mean to you? Inside the box on the left below, write down your own ideas about democracy and examples of democracy. Then, find definitions and examples of democracy in classroom and library resource books and write them down inside the box on the right. Compare the two lists. How are they similar and different?

My Own Ideas and Examples . . .

_____
_____
_____
_____
_____
_____
_____
_____
_____
_____
_____
_____

DEMOCRACY

Definitions and Examples from Books

_____
_____
_____
_____
_____
_____
_____
_____
_____
_____
_____
_____

Who Runs for President?

There are very few limitations on who can become president. The president must be at least 35 years old. He or she must also have been born in the United States and have lived in the United States country at least 14 years. With so few rules, the door is open for many people to qualify as a candidate for president.

Three quailifactions for president
- 35 years of age
- Born in the United States
- Have lived in the United States for at least 14 years

So how are candidates chosen from so many people that qualify? People who want to be president must become well-known. They are active in their local community. They take leadership roles in clubs. They become involved in volunteer work. They help plan parades, fairs, and other special events. The *public* begins to trust them as people who make good things happen.

The public also gets to know people who work in law or government. Many presidents were once lawyers. Many were *U.S. Senators* and Congressmen. Thus far, fourteen vice presidents and sixteen *governors* have become president. Lawyers and *politicians* often get their names in newspapers. They get exposure on TV news shows. People begin to listen to what they say.

Many people who want to be president begin by working for a *political party* for many years. They send out fliers. They make phone calls. They go door-to-door. They share their party's beliefs with others. They also tell people about others in their party who are running for office.

Every four years, we *elect* a president. Sometime before each election, people *announce* they would like to run for the job. Voters remember the work those people did in their towns. They remember seeing them on the news. They remember the work they did for their political parties.

The *major* parties vote to decide who will be their candidate. Members of smaller parties often hold meetings to decide on their candidate. Candidates who are not members of any party can run for president too. Sometimes voters write in a candidate who is not listed on the *ballot*.

Who Runs for President? ✮✮✮✮✮✮✮✮✮✮✮✮✮✮✮

public—people as a whole
governor—the head of a state
senator—a member of the Senate, a branch of government
politician—one who works in government
political party—a group of people who share similar views about how to run the
               country
elect—choose by voting for a candidate
announce—make known to the public
major—larger or greater
ballot—the means by which a person casts a vote

Use five of the vocabulary words above in sentences of your own.

1. _____

2. _____

3. _____

4. _____

5. _____

Questions to Consider

1. List the qualifications necessary to run for president. _____

   _____

   _____

2. People who want to become president do many things to become known by the
   public. List three of them. _____

   _____

3. How are candidates chosen? _____

   _____

4. Why do you think a person must be at least 35 to be the president?

   _____

   _____

The Running Mate ★★★★★★★★★★★★★★★★★★★

The vice president has only one *defined* duty. He is the head of the *Senate*. He is also only one step away from being president. When a president becomes *disabled*, the vice president takes over. When a president dies, the vice president immediately becomes president.

How is the right person chosen for the job? The *process* has changed down through the years. When our country was just beginning, the man who received the second greatest number of votes became vice president. That seemed like a good idea. But sometimes the president and vice president did not get along. They oftentimes did not come from the same political party. They didn't always agree on how the country should be run.

Then parties began to pick a *running mate* for their presidential candidate. They had their *electors* vote for a single *ticket*. The ticket listed both the president and vice president. This didn't always work either. Parties sometimes chose men who didn't get along. Other times, they chose vice presidents who would not make very good presidents if they had to take over the job.

Today party members still vote for a ticket, but the party doesn't choose the candidate for vice president. Presidential candidates choose their own running mates. They choose people with whom they can work. They try to choose people who will make voters happy. They try to choose people who share their goals. They also try to choose people who would become good presidents. Vice presidents have become president fourteen times in our nation's history.

50

The Running Mate ☆☆☆☆☆☆☆☆☆☆☆☆☆☆☆☆☆

Use each of the words defined here in sentences of your own.

defined—explained
Senate—one of our branches of government
disabled—to become unable to complete a task
process—the steps taken to complete a task
running mate—a candidate for vice president
electors—voters
ticket—a single ballot listing more than one candidate

1. _____

2. _____

3. _____

4. _____

5. _____

6. _____

7. _____

Questions to Consider

1. How was the vice president chosen when our country was just beginning?

   _____

2. Do you think it is a good idea to vote for the president and vice president on one ticket? Why or why not? _____

3. Why do you think the Constitution places the vice president in charge of the Senate? _____

   _____

4. Would you like to be the vice president? Why or why not?_____

   _____

5. Do you think it would be a good idea to make the first lady vice president? Explain your thoughts. _____

   _____

Who Can Vote? ✮✮✮✮✮✮✮✮✮✮✮✮✮✮✮✮✮✮

The United States is a *democracy*. That means we vote for our leaders. But not everyone has a voice in who becomes president. So, just who does get to vote? Many more people can vote today than once could!

Our Nation's First Voters

At first only white male landowners over 21 years old could vote in America. That meant four out of every five people were not allowed to vote In a true democracy, it became necessary to get the input of more voices. We also needed the input of more *varied* voices. Over the years, more and more people gained the right to vote.

Adding Voters

Six *amendments* to the Constitution have given the right to vote to more people. An amendment is a change or addition to the Constitution. The 14th Amendment (1868) says that voters do not have to own land. The 15th Amendment (1870) rules against race being a condition of having the right to vote. The 19th Amendment (1920) allows women to vote. The 23rd Amendment (1961) allows people who live in Washington, D.C. to vote for president. They were not able to before because they did not live in a state. The 24th Amendment (1964) says a voter cannot be charged money to be able to vote. The 26th Amendment (1971) lowered the voting age to 18. Each state decides who gets to vote. But their rules must not go against any of these amendments.

Today's Voters

Today there are only six main rules about who can vote. Voters must be 18 years old. They must be citizens of our country. They also must live in their state for 30 days before an election. In all states except North Dakota, voters must *register*. Having people sign up helps states keep track of who votes. The last two rules are *restrictions*. *Felons* cannot vote and neither can the mentally ill. Most adults in America can vote today and consider it is an honor to do so.

Name _____ Date _____

Who Can Vote? ★★★★★★★★★★★★★★★★★★★★

Read the definitions of the vocabulary words from the reading. Then unscramble them to complete the sentences below.

democracy—a country that allows its people to vote for its leaders
varied—showing variety
amendment—a change or addition
register—to sign up
restrictions—limits
felon—one who has committed a serious crime

1. In our (meoccyard) _____ we vote for our president.
2. Are you going to (rrgesite) _____ for the basketball team this year?
3. Karen made a slight (mmnneadte) _____ to her report.
4. Lisa made (riaved) _____ food choices when she selected a tuna salad, an apple, and a roll.
5. If you are a (nolef) _____ you cannot vote.
6. There are fewer (rsesntricito) _____ on voting than there once were.

Questions to Consider

Use each vocabulary word in a sentence of your own.

1. _____
2. _____
3. _____
4. _____
5. _____
6. _____

7. Who could vote in America during the days when our country had just begun?

   _____

8. What are the qualifications for voting in the United States today? _____

   _____

9. Have you ever voted for a student council member, or for and officer in a church election? Did your candidate win? _____

10. Why do you think the Constitution leaves it up to states to decide who can vote?

    _____

Who Does Vote? ★★★★★★★★★★★★★★★★★★★★

Women, *minorities*, and the poor had to fight for the right to vote. They struggled for years to change laws. Today elections are open to almost all citizens over the age of 18 years. Yet some people who qualify to vote, do not. In fact, less than half of the people who could vote usually do. Think about it. If fewer than half of the *eligible* voters vote, that means that fewer than half of the voting public speak for all Americans. That means less than half of the very different voices of American citizens are heard.

The Average Nonvoter

People who don't vote give different reasons for their choice. Some say they do not know enough about the people running for president. Others just don't prefer one *candidate* over the other. Some voters don't like the choice on their party's ticket. They think their *party* should have chosen someone else. Some people feel their vote does not make much difference. They apparently feel that one vote does not count for much.

The Average Voter

The average person who does vote fits a certain description. Most voters are older than 35. Most voters are married. The average voter went to school longer than the average nonvoter. Voters often make more money than those who don't vote. Most voters feel strong ties to a political party. They also think voting matters. Voters often read newspapers. They learn about the *issues*. They vote because they want to make a difference. They vote because they know it is the duty and *privilege* of a citizen of a democracy.

Voters Make a Difference

Voters do make a difference. President Grover Cleveland may have lost if more voters had gone to the *polls* in New York. Woodrow Wilson won only because Charles Hughes didn't get enough votes in California. The race between Thomas Dewey and Truman was so close that the news media thought

Dewey had won at first. The Kennedy–Nixon race was a close one. So was the Al Gore–George W. Bush election. In America today, most adults can vote. And every vote counts!

 How Our Government Works: Grade 5

Who Does Vote? ☆☆☆☆☆☆☆☆☆☆☆☆☆☆☆☆☆☆☆☆☆

Write a paragraph using these seven vocabulary words from the reading.

minority—less than 50 percent (In the United States, blacks are a
    minority.)

eligible—allowed to do something because requirements
    were met

candidate—one who is running for office

party—a political group

issue—a point people sometimes disagree about

privilege—a right that brings a special benefit

poll—a place where people vote

_____

_____

_____

_____

_____

Questions to Consider

1. Describe the average voter in America. _____

_____

_____

2. What reasons do people give for not voting? _____

_____

_____

3. List some close presidential races. _____

_____

_____

4. Why is it important to vote? _____

_____

_____

Getting Elected President ✮✮✮✮✮✮✮✮✮✮✮✮✮✮

Candidates for the presidency have a long and difficult path to travel before election day. To become the nominee of each major party, a candidate must win delegates to the national convention, which is held in mid-summer. Two imaginary candidates are profiled below. Based on the information provided, answer the questions below.

Candidate A

Name: Fred Johnson

Profile: age 46, married, three children, war veteran, business person, former senator

Positions: In favor of tax cuts, reducing federal budget, strong military, strong family values, being tough on criminals, and strong state governments.

Against excessive violence on TV and in films.

Candidate B

Name: Barbara North

Profile: age 51, married, one child, lawyer, former governor

Positions: In favor of improving education, federal programs to fight poverty, gun control, strengthening America's role as a world leader, and enhancing civil rights.

Against cutting needed federal programs for needy and prayer in schools.

1. Write a brief description of Candidate A based upon the information provided.

   _____

   _____

   _____

2. Write a brief description of Candidate B based upon the information provided.

   _____

   _____

   _____

3. Which candidate do you prefer? _____

   Why? _____

   _____

   _____

The Electoral College ✫✫✫✫✫✫✫✫✫✫✫✫✫✫✫

The electoral college was created by the Constitution. It is a group of delegates chosen by the voters to elect the president and vice president. On election day, the first Tuesday after the first Monday in November, voters mark a ballot for president and vice president. They do not actually vote for the candidates, but they select electors, or delegates, to represent their state in the electoral college. Each state has as many votes in the electoral college as it has senators and representatives.
There are 538 electors. The electors meet in December on a date set by law to cast their votes. The results are sent to the president of the Senate who opens them. A candidate must receive 270 or a majority of the electoral votes to win. After two representatives from each body of Congress have counted the electoral votes, the results are officially announced in January. The public knows the results right after the November election because the news media figures them out. These results are not official until the electoral votes have been counted by Congress. A candidate may win the popular vote but lose the election.

Answer true or false to the following statements. The letters in parentheses in the true answers spell out the names of the two presidents who lost the popular vote but won the election.

_____ 1. The electo(r)al res(u)l(t)s are announced in January.

_____ 2. The Founding Fat(h)ers did not want Congr(e)ss to select the p(r)esident.

_____ 3. Each state (h)as the same numb(e)r of electors.

_____ 4. The (f)irst Tuesday after the first M(o)nday in Novembe(r) is Election (D)ay.

_____ 5. Decem(b)er is w(h)en the elector(a)l college meets.

_____ 6. Voters actuall(y) vote for the d(e)legate(s).

_____ 7. Congress (a)nd the public (n)ominate the cand(i)date(s).

_____ 8. A (b)allot is mark(e)d by voters in (N)ovember.

_____ 9. A ma(j)ority of elector(a)l votes (m)akes a w(i)n(n)er.

_____ 10. T(h)ere (a)re five hund(r)ed thi(r)ty-e(i)ght elector(s).

_____ 11. The electi(o)n for preside(n)t is t(h)e first Tu(e)sday in Decembe(r).

_____ 12. It takes 270 elect(o)ral votes to wi(n) the presidency.

The two presidents are _____ and _____.

Democrats and Republicans ✫✫✫✫✫✫✫✫✫✫✫

America's two major parties are the Democrats and the Republicans. Both parties have *national committees*. These are groups of people who work for the party. Committee members work to get the message of the party out. They remind others to vote. Each committee spreads a somewhat different message.

The Republicans

The Republicans started out as a *third party* in 1856. In that year, they supported John C. Fremont for president. Fremont stood behind two beliefs. He thought slaves should be freed. He also thought people who settled the West should not have to pay for their land. Fremont did not win the election, but he did get one-third of the votes. By the next election, the Republicans were a major party. Their candidate, Abraham Lincoln, won the White House in 1860.

The Republican *platform* states what the party stands for. Republicans believe in the freedom for all people. They think it is important to have a strong sense of pride in our nation. They have a goal of spending our country's money wisely. They want to see American businesses succeed. Republicans believe town and state laws are helpful in solving local problems.

The Democrats

The Democratic Party grew out of the Democratic-Republicans. The party was formed by Thomas Jefferson. It was known as the "party of the common man." The Democrats still honor the common man. Democratic presidents have started programs that help people. Jefferson fought for the *Bill of Rights* to be included in the Constitution. The Bill of Rights is the first ten amendments to the Constitution. They give certain rights to people in our country. Franklin Roosevelt started *Social Security*. Social Security is a program that provides money to older people. President Kennedy started the Peace Corps. The Peace Corps gives jobs to young people who want to help the world. The Civil Rights Act passed under President Lyndon B. Johnson. That act makes sure people of all races are treated fairly.

Both of America's main parties want the best for our country. It is good that the parties have different focuses. Voters can see that there is more than one way to make our country great.

Name _____   Date _____

Democrats and Republicans ✮✮✮✮✮✮✮✮✮✮✮✮

Use the reading to help you match the vocabulary words with their definitions.

1. national committees
2. third party
3. platform
4. Bill of Rights
5. Social Security

a. a minor political party
b. a program that provides money to older people
c. groups of people who work for political parties
d. states what a group stands for
e. the first ten amendments to the Constitution

Questions to Consider

1. What are the beliefs of the Republican Party? _____

_____

2. What beliefs are supported by the Democratic Party? _____

_____

3. What do members of national committees do? _____

_____

4. If you could choose to be a member of the Republican or Democratic Party, which would you choose and why?

_____

_____

_____

_____

_____

_____

_____

Third-Party Power ★★★★★★★★★★★★★★★★★★★

Some voters in America do not belong to a main party. Some belong to no party. Others are members of a third party. Third parties have a lot fewer members than Republicans or Democrats. There are several third parties in America. Each has its own goals. Third parties elect *officials* at city and state levels. Some of them also run candidates for president. No third-party candidate has yet become president. Three of the larger third parties are the Reform Party, the Libertarians, and the Green Party.

Reform Party

The Reform Party was *formed* by Ross Perot in 1992. Perot is a Texas billionaire. He wanted to be president. There have been many other leaders in the Reform Party since 1992. There have also been arguments, so the party is smaller today than it once was.

Some members left to form the Constitution Party. The Constitution Party does not like *welfare*, taxes, or *immigration*. They want to allow children to pray in school.

Some who left the Reform Party formed the America First Party. They like laws that make trading with other countries less difficult. They believe we should have strong families and a strong faith. They think some lawmakers are not making fair decisions. They want to clean up Washington.

Libertarian Party

The Libertarian Party was formed in 1971. It was once the largest third party. The Libertarians believe people should be free to make their own choices. They think lawmakers make too many of those choices today. They support home schools. They do not support rules about who can own guns. They think people should pay less taxes. They do not think we should have a welfare system.

Green Party

Green Party members are concerned about the health of the planet. They support *recycling*. They think using *solar* power is better than using oil. They like when countries work together to protect the earth. They support laws that help the planet. The Green Party nominated Ralph Nader for president in 2000. He finished third.

Third-Party Power ✫✫✫✫✫✫✫✫✫✫✫✫✫✫✫✫✫✫✫

Complete the sentences below with words from the vocabulary list.

official—person in charge or in office
formed—created, made
welfare—a system that provides money and food to the poor
immigration—the movement of people from one country to another
recycling—reusing
solar—energy from the sun

1. The _____ of Europeans to America began before the first president was elected.

2. Your state senator is an elected _____.

3. Grandma went on _____ when she ran out of money after losing her job.

4. Our school has a _____ center where we collect bottles, cans, newspapers, and plastic.

5. My friends and I _____ a band and played at school events.

6. Our school swimming pool is heated with _____ panels that collect the sun's heat.

Questions to Consider

1. What party was started by Ross Perot in 1992? _____

_____

2. What two parties were born out of the Reform Party? _____

_____

3. What is the main message of the Libertarian Party? _____

_____

4. What is the main message of the Green Party?_____

_____

5. Who ran for president on the Green Party ticket in 2000? _____

_____

Campaigning Throughout History ★★★★★★★★★

George Washington did not campaign for his job. The public wanted him to lead the young nation. Several presidents after him didn't campaign either, but for different reasons.

Early Campaigns

Candidates could not reach all voters at the start of our nation. There were no planes, trains, or cars. There were no telephones, TVs, radios, or computers. But these are not the only reasons candidates didn't campaign. They didn't campaign for another reason. It was thought *undignified* to brag about yourself. Instead, others did the bragging. *Supporters* campaigned for the person they wanted to win. Supporters knew they could not reach all voters in the early days, so they focused on cities. Many voters learned little about the candidates before an election.

Changing Attitudes

Andrew Jackson's 1828 campaign was different. His supporters were the first to try and reach all voters. They sent stories to newspapers. They put up posters and they planned rallies in both large and small towns.

The election of 1840 added another *tactic* to campaigning. William Henry Harrison's supporters tried to dazzle voters. They wrote catchy *slogans*. They planned parades and they hired bands to perform.

By the 1860 campaign, candidates finally spoke for themselves. Both Abraham Lincoln and Stephen Douglas made themselves *visible*. They were the first candidates to debate each other in public.

New Inventions

Jackson, Harrison, Douglas, and Lincoln changed public attitudes toward campaigning. New inventions carried the attitudes to the whole nation. James Polk spread the news of his candidacy by telegraph in 1844. William Jennings Bryan ran for president from the back of a train. By 1896, railroad tracks connected the country from coast to coast, so Bryan hopped on. He rode over 18,000 miles and made more than 600 speeches. He reached the ears of 5,000 voters. Candidates began to use the radio in 1924. *Motorcades* were added to campaigns in 1928. The 1952 elections made use of both TV and airplanes.

Modern candidates have countless past plans to draw from when they decide how to campaign today.

Campaigning Throughout History ✯✯✯✯✯✯✯✯

Read the definitions of the vocabulary words below.
Then decide which word comes to mind when you
read each description below.

undignified—having no dignity or honor
supporter—a person who votes for and/or otherwise
         helps a candidate get elected
tactic—action or plan
slogan—a catchy phrase meant to give a candidate
a good image
visible—able to be seen
motorcade—a number of cars traveling together

_____ 1. Al Gore's photo was on billboards, in newspapers, and on TV.

_____ 2. "Bring Back Common Sense."

_____ 3. Name-calling in a presidential campaign ad.

_____ 4. Kennedy and his advisors paraded into town in black limousines.

_____ 5. Bryan tried stop in all towns along railroad tracks and talking to people.

_____ 6. Uncle Jim displays a poster for his favorite candidate in his yard.

Questions to Consider

1. Why did candidates not campaign in the early presidential elections? _____

   _____

2. Why was it difficult for candiates to reach all voters before the late 1800s? _____

   _____

3. Who first added parades, bands, and slogans to campaigning? _____

   _____

4. William Jennings Bryan never became president. Still, his campaign is famous.
   Why?_____

   _____

5. Lincoln and Douglas were the first candidates to do what?_____

   _____

Election Day ☆☆☆☆☆☆☆☆☆☆☆☆☆☆☆☆☆☆☆☆☆

A president is elected every four years. The Tuesday after the first Monday in November is Election Day. Campaigning is over on Election Day, but many people are still very busy.

The Candidates

The candidates vote in their hometowns. Then, with family and friends, they focus on news reports. They watch election *figures* change as people go to the polls, which open very early in the morning and close at 7:00 P.M. Late election night results are reported. The losing candidate thanks his or her supporters and congratulates the winner. The winning candidate thanks his or her supporters, too. Then he or she gives a *victory* speech. Both candidates study election results. Doing so helps them in future contests.

The Voters

Most voters' *polling places* are in schools, churches, or other public buildings. Some voters mark paper ballots. Others punch holes in ballots that computers can read. Many pull handles on voting machines that keep track of votes as they are made. In Oregon, voters mark ballots that are mailed to them. They must return the ballots by Election Day. Voters who are out of their state or out of the country on Election Day can mail in *absentee ballots*.

Party Workers

Party workers are not done with their chores on Election Day. Some call party members and remind them to vote. Others drive older voters to the polls or baby-sit for young parents who wish to vote. Party workers keep track of who votes during the day. They call those who have not voted by evening and remind them to do so.

Election Judges

Poll watchers *assure* that elections are *conducted* fairly. They check voters' names and addresses. They make sure only qualified voters vote and they make sure no one votes twice. They must also ensure that no qualified voter is stopped from voting. They do not allow anyone to campaign in polling places, or even bring in newspapers and radios. Late at night, they count votes and report them to state *officials*.

Television Newscasters

TV news programs report election results. They list election figures on a huge scoreboard. Figures are listed for each state. Newscasters update figures as new results come in. Between updates, they interview experts. They comment on results and make *predictions* about who will win. They even report from party headquarters and candidate homes or hotels.

Election Day is a busy day for candidates, voters, workers, and reporters alike.

Election Day ✮✮✮✮✮✮✮✮✮✮✮✮✮✮✮✮✮✮✮✮✮✮✮✮✮

Unscramble the vocabulary words to learn their definitions

1. yctoivr—a win _____

2. Ingopli cepsal—where voters cast their ballots _____

3. beesaetn slotlab—votes cast through the mail _____

4. rigseuf—numbers or calculations _____

5. lcfioiafs—people in authority _____

6. cctoenddu—managed _____

7. tdiocrenip—a guess about the future _____

8. sreasu—guarantee _____

Questions to Consider

1. What are the duties of the following people on Election Day?

   The candidates _____

   _____

   The voters _____

   _____

   Party workers _____

   _____

   Election Judges _____

   _____

   Television newscasters _____

2. Why is it important to have election judges at polling places? _____

   _____

3. Why does it take so long to get the final results of an election? _____

   _____

4. Why do candidates analyze the election results. _____

   _____

Electing Our Presidents in the Future ★★★★★★

Our election *process* has changed over the years. How will it change in the future?

Campaign Changes

Many people would like to see changes in campaigns. They don't think they should be so expensive. They don't want special interest groups giving candidates *funds*. They don't want businesses doing so either.

Some people don't like the role of television in political campaigns. They say TV coverage forces candidates to focus on *image* instead of *issues*. They also argue that *commentaries* affect voters too much. They think voters don't vote based on facts anymore. They vote based on the opinions of news reports and images created on television.

In the future, we could see campaigns that cost less. Rules about where campaign money comes from could be changed. We could also see changes in TV's role in elections.

Voting Changes

Some people think we should change the way we vote for president. They say we should get rid of the Electoral College. They want the people to vote directly.

Others suggest other changes in the way we vote. They would like to see citizens *required* to vote. Today, less than half of the *qualified* voters vote in most elections. If our country is to be run by the people, the people need to vote.

Some people think more people would vote if we made it easier. They remind us that in some countries the polls are open on weekends. That's when most people are not at work. In some countries, the polls are open for more than just one day. Some states are starting to make voting easy by allowing their voters to mail in their ballots. Other states offer early voting days. Others are pushing for future elections to be decided by voters making their choices over the Internet.

Others hope for more choices at the polls. They would like third-party candidates to have a fair chance at winning. They would also like to see women and minorities on the ballot.

Whatever the changes, the future is sure to be as exciting as the past in the world of presidential elections!

Electing Our Presidents in the Future ✰✰✰✰✰✰

Use context clues from the reading or a dictionary to help you match the vocabulary words with their definitions.

1. _____ process
2. _____ funds
3. _____ commentaries
4. _____ image
5. _____ issue
6. _____ required
7. _____ qualified

a. money
b. insisted on or made necessary
c. opinions given by a news person or expert
d. a concern
e. a mental or actual picture
f. steps taken to reach a goal
g. meeting the rules or limits for doing something

Questions to Consider

8. What campaign changes might we see in the future? Why do some people want them? _____

_____

_____

9. What voting changes might we see in the future? Why do some people want them? _____

_____

_____

10. Why does it take a long time to make big changes? _____

_____

_____

11. How might the president's job change in the future? _____

_____

_____

Electoral College?????

Name _____   Date _____

Evaluating Political Messages ★★★★★★★★★★★★

How influential are the media on American political
life? The chart below lists some major opportunities
the media provide for individuals to communicate
their concerns and positions on current issues. Search
for examples of each of them on TV and radio, on
the Internet (under teacher and/or parental
supervision), and in current newspapers, news
magazines, and other print sources. Then for each
one, identify the concern and position inside the
boxes on the chart.

Media & Format	Concern	Position
Letter to the Editor		
TV Talk Show		
Radio Talk Show		
Opinion/Editorial Page		
Public Opinion Poll		
Newsletter		
Internet		

Political Dictionary ✮✮✮✮✮✮✮✮✮✮✮✮✮✮✮✮✮✮

How is your political vocabulary? Below on the right is a list of vocabulary words that every politically savvy person ought to know. The column on the left lists the definitions for those words. Your task is to use classroom or library reference books to match the words and definitions correctly.

_____ 1. a statement of government policy

_____ 2. to impose or collect money required by the government, such as income tax

_____ 3. an independent politician; in 1884, one who left the Republican Party

_____ 4. a group of electors that elects the president and vice president of the United States

_____ 5. related and limited to one's own country

_____ 6. dividing district boundaries to give one party the political advantage

_____ 7. government official skilled in negotiation

_____ 8. executive power to stop legislative measure

_____ 9. to get more votes than the other candidates, but less than a majority (50% or more) of the votes

_____ 10. officer in charge of legislative body

_____ 11. unofficial, but often influential, advisors

_____ 12. a member of the electoral college

_____ 13. Closed meeting of political party

_____ 14. helps organize and unify his/her party's legislators

_____ 15. a little known contestant for political office

_____ 16. appointments made in exchange for political favors

_____ 17. a representative at a party convention

A. electoral college

B. plurality

C. whip

D. domestic

E. gerrymandering

F. levy

G. caucus

H. Speaker

I. elector

J. Kitchen Cabinet

K. dark horse

L. veto

M. diplomat

N. spoils system

O. mugwump

P. delegate

Q. doctrine

Answer Key ★★★★★★★★★★★★★★★★★★★★★

Page 6 ....**What's It For?**

Answers will vary.

Page 7 ....**Framers of the Constitution**

1. Philadelphia

2. 55

3. half were lawyers and judges, one fourth were landowners, all had held one public office, and all were wealthy

4. to recommend changes in government

5. no, because they had different opinions about the best government

6. Franklin

7. Washington

8. Constitutional Convention

9. Madison

10. The new Constitution proposed a powerful executive and a Senate with powers equal to those of the House.

Page 8 ....**In Your Own Words**

1. form a more perfect Union

2. establish Justice

3. insure Tranquility

4. provide for defense

5. promote general Welfare

6. secure Liberty

Page 9 ....**Amendment Matchup**

A. 21st

B. 14th

C. 24th

D. 13th

E. 26th

F. 19th

G. 22nd

H. 17th

I. 25th

J. 15th

K. 20th

L. 18th

M. 23rd

N. 11th

O. 12th

P. 27th

Q. 16th

Page 10 ....**Amending the Constitution**

1. V

2. an amendment

Answers will vary.

Page 11 ....**Functions of Government**

Answers will vary.

Page 12......................Rights and Responsibilities

1. right
2. right
3. right
4. responsibility
5. right
6. right
7. right
8. right
9. responsibility
10. responsibility
11. responsibility
12. responsibility
13. responsibility
14 right
15. right
16. responsibility
17. right

Page 13 ....Democratic Quiz

Answers will vary.

Page 14.............................Protecting Your Rights

1. F
2. G
3. D
4. I
5. C
6. B
7. H
8. J
9. E
10. A

Page 15 ....Citizen Checklist

Answers will vary.

Page 16 ....American Society

Answers will vary.

Page 17..............................Who Represents You?

Answers will vary.

Page 18...........................Government in Your Life

Answers will vary.

Answer Key ★★★★★★★★★★★★★★★★★★★★

Page 19 ....Forms of Government

1. In presidential powers are shared; in parliamentary power rests in the legislative branch.

2. In confederal each state is sovereign; in federal powers are shared between national and states; and in parliamentary the head of government is chosen from the ranks of the majority party.

Page 20 ....Community Needs

Answers will vary.

Page 21 ....Asking the Right Questions

Answers will vary.

Page 22 ....Community Resources

Answers will vary.

Page 23 ....A Federal System

1. N
2. N
3. S
4. N
5. N
6. S
7. S
8. S
9. N
10. N
11. N
12. S
13. N
14. S
15. N
16. S
17. N
18. N

Page 24 ....Branches of Government

Legislative Branch: • impeach the president • pass laws over the president's veto by two-thirds majority vote of both Houses • establish committees to oversee activities of executive branch • disapprove appointments made by the president • propose amendments to the U.S. Constitution

Executive Branch: • nominate members of the federal judiciary • veto laws passed by Congress

Judicial Branch: • overrule decisions made by lower courts • declare laws made by Congress to be unconstitutional • declare actions of the executive branch to be unconstitutional

Page 25.....Organization of the U.S. Government

1. E
2. J
3. L
4. E
5. L
6. L
7. J
8. E
9. E
10. J
11. E
12. L
13. L
14. J
15. L
16. E
17. J
18. L
19. J

Page 26 ....Domestic Policies

Answers will vary.

Page 27.............................Foreign Policy

Answers will vary.

Page 28 ....All About the House

1. E
2. B
3. H
4. J
5. A
6. M
7. C
8. P
9. G
10. N

Page 29 ....Senate Facts

1. smaller
2. two
3. state
4. 100
5. upper chamber
6. revenue
7. treaties
8. appointment
9. legislature
10. seventeenth
11. voters
12. six
13. state
14. Constitution
15. president
16. tie
17. pro tempore

Answer Key ★★★★★★★★★★★★★★★★★★★★★★★

Page 30 ....Comparing Houses of Congress

Senate	House of Representatives
100	435
by voters in state	by voters in district
senator	representative
whole state	district
age: 30, 9-year citizen, resident of state	age: 25, 7-year citizen, resident of state
6 years	2 years
president	speaker of the House
Answers will vary.	Answers will vary.
Senate convicts	House impeaches
approves treaties and certain appointments	originates tax bills

Page 31 ....Making Laws

A. 8
B. 6
C. 2
D. 3
E. 1
F. 4
G. 9
H. 5
I. 7

Page 32 ....The Judicial Branch

1. national
2. the Constitution
3. judicial
4. federal, state, local
5. justice

Page 33 ....The Supreme Court

Answers will vary.

Page 34 ......Important Supreme Court Decisions

1. E
2. I
3. F
4. B
5. D
6. C
7. A
8. J
9. G
10. H

Page 35 ....The Executive Branch

1. 4 years
2. vice president
3. Born a citizen of the United States, at least 35 years old, have been a resident of the United States at least 14 years.
4. the following should be checked: c, d, e, h, i
5. Student's should write the oath of office (found on page 38.)

Page 37.........................The Job of the President

Answers will vary.

Questions to Consider (answers will vary)

1. The president is the chief diplomat, the head of the armed forces, and the enforcer of laws.

2. He meets with leaders of other countries, attends dinners and meetings, and makes treaties.

3. He talks to leaders of our military and decides when to send troops to war and when to call them home again.

4. The president chooses judges and cabinet members, signs or vetoes bills, and heads the police force.

5.–6. Student opinion should be well-supported.

Page 39...........................Presidency Fill-In

1. chief executive
2. enforce
3. foreign
4. defense
5. party
6. judicial
7. justices
8. White House
9. cabinet
10. Congress
11. four
12. twice

Page 38..................................Presidential Power

1. T
2. F
3. T
4. F
5. T
6. T
7. T
8. T
9. F
10. F
11. T
12. F
13. F
14. T
15. F
16. T
17. F
18. F

Page 40......................................Cabinet Officers

Check current source for names.

Answer Key ☆☆☆☆☆☆☆☆☆☆☆☆☆☆☆☆☆☆☆☆☆

Page 41.................**Checks and Balances Chart**

The President may	The Supreme Court may	Congress may
pass or veto it	declare the law unconstitutional	
		override the veto with a 2/3 vote
		the Senate may approve or disapprove the appointment
		impeach the judge
		the Senate may approve or disapprove the treaty
	declare the law unconstitutional	
		may not give it to the president

Page 42 ....**Powerful Ideas**

1. E
2. G
3. I
4. B
5. D
6. H
7. C
8. A
9. F
10. J

Page 43 ....A Limited and Unlimited Government

Limited: • regular and free elections, • independent judiciaries, • protection of individual rights, • protection from government, • multiple political parties, • laws apply to leaders as well as the governed, • goals and

means of government cannot violate constitution, Great Britain, Canada, France

Unlimited: • courts controlled by leader, • no restraints on government, • no free elections, • government use of intimidation and terror, Soviet Union, Iran, Libya, Italy under Mussolini, Myanmar, China

Page 44 ....Dictatorships and Democracies

Dictatorships	Democracies
not allowed to disagree with the government	allowed to disagree with the government
elections controlled by the government	fair and free elections
led by all-powerful leader	none
none	led by elected officials
serve the government	government serves individual

How Our Government Works: Grade 5

Page 45 ....**Comparative Governments**

1. E
2. I
3. F
4. H
5. D
6. J
7. L
8. G
9. B
10. C
11. K
12. A

Answers will vary.

Page 46.............**The United States and the World**

Answers will vary.

Page 47 ....**The Meaning of Democracy**

Answers will vary.

Page 49 ....**Who Runs for President?**

Accept complete sentences that show understanding of each word.

Questions to Consider (answers will vary)

1. A presidential candidate must be at least 35 years old, born in the United States, and lived in the country at least 14 years.

2. Presidential hopefuls make speeches, make phone calls, and campaign for others in their party.

3. Presidential candidates are selected by the votes of political party members or through discussions at party meetings.

4. Perhaps the president is required to be 35 or older so that he is both experienced and mature.

Page 51 ....**The Running Mate**

Accept complete sentences that show understanding of each word.

Questions to Consider (answers will vary)

1. The vice president was the man who got the second most votes in Presidential Elections.

2.–5. Student opinion should be well-supported.

Answer Key ★★★★★★★★★★★★★★★★★★★★★★

Page 53 ....Who Can Vote?

1. democracy   2. register   3. amendment

4. varied   5. felon   6. restrictions

7.–12. Student sentences should show understanding of the words.

Questions to Consider (answers will vary)

1. In the beginning, only white male landowners over 21 could vote.

2. Citizens of the United States who are at least 18 years old, are registered to vote, and have lived in their state for 30 days before an election can vote today.

3. Answers will vary.

4. States might be responsible for deciding who votes because each state has its own unique population and issues of concern. The Constitution's framers may also have been trying to give states' rights supporters more leverage when they decided to leave voting rules up to the states.

Page 55 ....Who Does Vote?

Accept a complete paragraph that shows understanding of the words.

Questions to Consider (answers will vary)

1. The average American voter is a married person over 35 who is wealthier and more educated than the average nonvoter. The average voter is informed and interested in the election.

2. People choose not to vote because they do not know the candidates; they do not like the choices; or they do not think they can make a difference.

3. Close races include those between Wilson and Hughes, Dewey and Truman, Kennedy and Nixon, and Gore and Bush.

4. Many elections are close, so it is important to vote for the candidate whose ideas you support. It is our civic duty to vote as members of a democracy.

Page 56 ....Getting Elected President

Answers will vary.

Page 57 ....The Electoral College

1. T

2. T

3. F

4. T

5. T

6. T

7. F

8. T

9. T

10. T

11. F

12. T

Rutherford B. Hayes; Benjamin Harrison

Page 59 ....Democrats and Republicans

1. c   2. a   3. d   4. e   5. b

Questions to Consider (answers will vary)

1. Republicans have a goal of spending money wisely and supporting businesses. They believe in the freedom of all people and the importance of having pride in the country. They believe local and state governments can often solve local problems best.

2. Democrats support the "common person." Many of the laws and programs they put in place address social concerns.

3. National committee members work to get the message and the vote out for the party.

4. Student responses should be well supported.

Page 61................................Third-Party Power

1. immigration 2. official 3. welfare
4. recycling 5. formed 6. solar

Questions to Consider (answers will vary)

1. Ross Perot started the Reform Party.

2. The Constitution Party and America First Party evolved from the Reform Party.

3. The main message of the Libertarian Party is that individuals should be free to make their own choices.

4. The main message of the Green Party is that government decisions need to take into account the affect the decisions have on the planet.

5. Ralph Nader was the Green Party presidential candidate in 2000.

Page 63 ....Campaigning Throughout History

1. visible 2. slogan 3. undignified
4. motorcade 5. tactic 6. supporter

Questions to Consider (answers will vary)

1. It was considered undignified.

2. Modern modes of transportation and means of communication were not yet available.

3. William Henry Harrison was the first to use parades, bands, and slogans.

4. His campaign is famous due to the thousands of miles he traveled and hundreds of speeches he gave.

5. They were the first to debate in public.

Page 65 ....Election Day

1. victory 2. polling places 3. absentee ballots
4. figures 5. officials 6. conducted 7. prediction
8. assure

Questions to Consider (answers will vary)

1. The candidates vote in their hometowns and watch election results as they are tallied. The voters vote. Party workers get people to the polls. Election judges assure the election is conducted fairly. Television newscasters report and comment on results, interview experts and candidates, and make predictions.

2. Election results require additional time because people can vote all day long until the polls close in the early evening.

3. Candidates analyze results so they have a better chance of winning the next time.

Page 67 ....Electing Our President in the Future

1. f 2. a 3. c 4. f 5. e 6. b 7. g

Questions to Consider (answers will vary)

1. Campaign changes could include lowering the cost, new rules about funding, and limits on TV coverage. People want changes because campaign costs are high and funded by groups that may get favors. Also, TV coverage creates an image rather than an issues campaign.

2. Voter changes could include requiring citizens to vote, making voting easier, getting rid of the Electoral College, and adding minorities and women to the ticket. Voters want changes to make voting more democratic and to include more voters and more choices.

3.-4. Student opinion should be well supported.

Page 68 ....Evaluating Political Messages

Answers will vary.

Answer Key ★★★★★★★★★★★★★★★★★★★★★★★★

Page 69 ....Political Dictionary

1. Q
2. F
3. O
4. A
5. D
6. E
7. M
8. L
9. B
10. H
11. J
12. I
13. G
14. C
15. K
16. N
17. P